Starting
Face Painting

Fiona Watt and Caro Childs

Designed by Non Figg

Illustrated by Kevin Lyle
Photography by Ray Moller

Additional photography by Howard Allman
With thanks to John Russell

Contents

Things you need

Before you begin to paint the faces in this book, you will need to have a few special things. You can buy them all from a theatrical suppliers or costume shop. Some large toy stores also sell them. You don't need to buy lots of paints at first because you can mix them like ordinary paint to make different shades.

Paints

All the faces in this book are painted with water-based face paints. You can buy them in individual pots or in a box or palette.

Brushes

You will need to have one thin brush and one thick one. Another kind of brush which is good for face painting is one with a flat end.

Sponges

You use a sponge to cover large areas with face paint. You can use a make-up sponge or cut pieces from an ordinary bath sponge.

Face paints in a palette

Pots of face paints

Make-up sponge

Special face painting sponge

Thin brush with pointed tip

Flat-ended brush

Thick brush

Bath sponge

You will also need an old mug or jam jar for cleaning your brush.

Test the paint

If you have sensitive skin, put a patch of face paint on your hand. Leave it for an hour or so to see if you react to it.

An old plate or saucer for mixing paints.

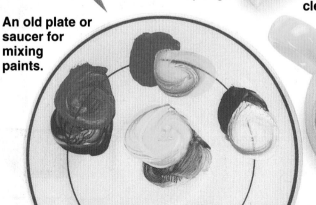

Helpful tips

This keeps your hand steady as you paint.

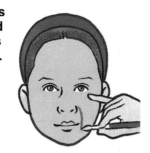

Wash it off

Put one hand on top of your model's head. This helps you to turn their head as you paint.

Put your little finger on your model's face, near to the place you are going to start painting.

Paint a line, keeping your finger on the face. Turn your hand slowly as you are painting.

When you want to take off your face paint, wash it off with a wet cotton ball and mild soap.

Sitting comfortably

It's important that you, and the person you are painting, are sitting comfortably. Put your paints and water pot for cleaning your brush where you can reach them.

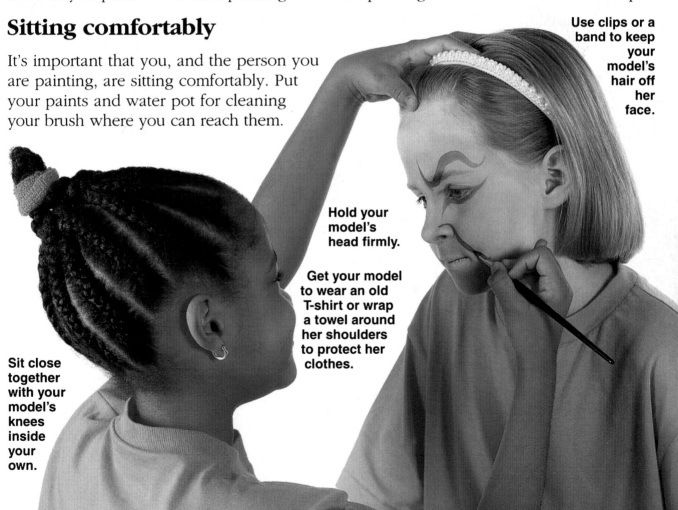

Use clips or a band to keep your model's hair off her face.

Hold your model's head firmly.

Get your model to wear an old T-shirt or wrap a towel around her shoulders to protect her clothes.

Sit close together with your model's knees inside your own.

Starting out

For a link to a website where you can find some simple face-painting ideas from around the world, go to **www.usborne-quicklinks.com**

Before you begin to paint anybody's face, make sure that you have all the things you need and that your model is comfortable. The faces on these pages are very easy to paint. They will help you to get used to painting different shapes and simple patterns.

Putting paint on your brush

Hold your brush just above the bristles.

1. Hold your brush in your fingers, like a pencil. Dip its bristles into a jar of clean water.

2. Roll your brush around and around in one of your face paints. Don't press too hard.

3. If your brush isn't wet enough to mix the paint, dip it into the water again, then roll it in the paint.

You can paint one shade on top of another. Wait until the first one is dry before painting on top.

Try to keep each line as even as you can.

4. Add more water until you have a 'puddle' of face paint mixed with water.

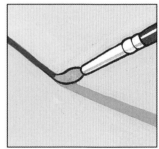

5. When you paint, you need to hold your brush at an angle away from the face, like this.

Painting a line

Red and orange show up well if your skin is pale.

You could add a line across the cheeks.

1. Place your little finger on your model's face. Try not to grip your brush too tightly.

2. Paint a line without lifting your brush. Turn your hand, but leave your finger on the face.

3. Put more paint on your brush, before you do another line. Wash it if you use a different shade.

Simple stripes

1. With yellow on your brush, paint a thick line across the forehead, without lifting your brush.

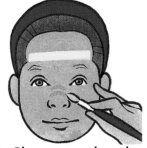

2. Clean your brush. Put green face paint onto a brush and paint two green lines over the nose.

3. Dip a thin brush in red and paint a zigzag line across each cheek. Start near the mouth.

5

Glitter and jewels

It's easy to brighten up a simple pattern by adding glitter paint and jewels on top of your face paint. You can buy these from theatrical suppliers or costume shops. You'll also need special glue or petroleum jelly for sticking on your jewels.

Glitter paint

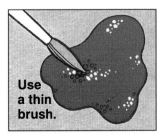

Use a thin brush.

Squeeze a little glitter paint onto the back of your hand. Dip the tip of a very clean brush into it.

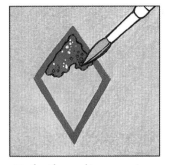

Dab the glittery tip gently onto your model's face. The gel around the glitter will dry.

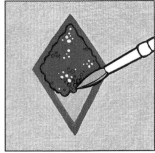

Fill in your shape by dabbing the tip in the glitter lots of times. Don't try to brush it on thickly.

Your jewel needs to be flat on the back.

Jewels

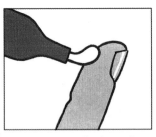

Squeeze a little of the special glue onto your finger. Dab it where you want your jewel to go.

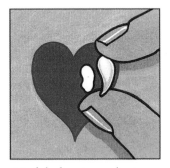

Hold the jewel at the edges and press it gently onto the glue. Don't touch it while the glue dries.

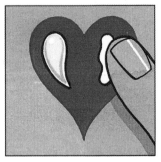

If you use petroleum jelly, dab a little on your forehead. Press the jewel into it. The jelly doesn't dry.

Simple-shaped jewels look best.

Most glitter paint comes in a gel in a tube. You don't need to mix it with water.

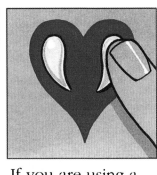

If you are using a self-adhesive jewel, you need to wait until the face paint is dry, then press it on.

For a link to a website where you can find out how to make a princess tiara to go with your face paint, go to **www.usborne-quicklinks.com**

Prince and princesses

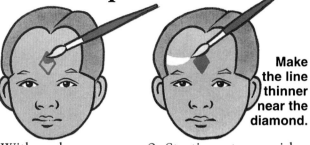

Use a flat-ended brush.

Make the line thinner near the diamond.

Use a thin brush.

1. With red on your brush, paint a diamond in the middle of the forehead. Fill it in.

2. Starting at one side of the forehead, paint a white line to the diamond. Do one on the other side too.

3. Hold the brush with the bristles like this and paint some small red diamonds on the lines.

4. Paint black lines around all the diamonds. Add small dots along the white line, too.

Wear lipstick or paint red face paint on your lips.

Add dots of glitter paint along the lines and on your cheeks.

Add white 'sparkle' lines around your jewels.

Paint a heart shape instead of a diamond.

Matching sides

With some faces, it's important to try to get both sides to look the same. If you go wrong, you can't rub out face paint, but you can add more to make the shapes match.

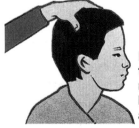

Don't twist the model's body around.

Turn the head so that the side you are painting is facing you.

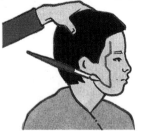

Use a straw to add tiny circles around the helmet (see right).

Paint an outline of a shape. You can fill it in later when you are sure that both sides are the same.

Fill in the cheeks and forehead on a face like this, when both sides look the same.

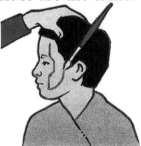

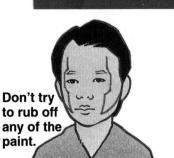

Don't try to rub off any of the paint.

When you have done one side, turn the head so that the other side faces you. Paint it carefully.

Look at the face from the front. Do the sides match? Add more paint in places if you need to.

Filling in

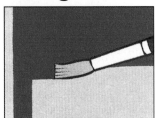

When you fill in a shape, use a thick brush. Brush on the paint in lines which touch each other.

Mix enough paint to cover the shape you are filling in.

To stop the shape from being streaky, try to keep the paint the same thickness for the whole shape.

Paint any pattern you like on the badge on your helmet.

Space cop

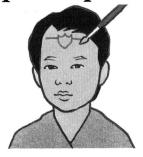

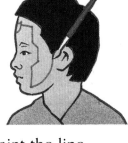

1. Put red onto a thin brush. Paint a badge shape on the forehead. Add a line across like this.

2. Paint the line down the side of the face, nearly to the chin. Take it back up across the cheek.

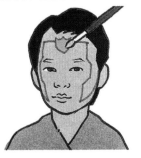

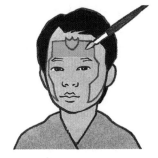

3. Copy the same shape on the other side of the face. Fill the badge in with silver paint.

4. Paint a silver line across the eyebrows. Fill in the shape between this line and the red one.

Using a straw

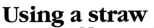

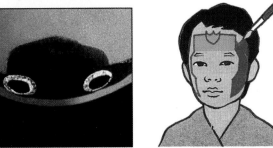

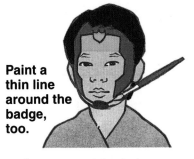

Paint a thin line around the badge, too.

For a small circle, dip a drinking straw into your paint. Press it gently on your hand to test it.

If you are doing a circle on a dark paint, like on the face above, use a light shade of paint.

5. Fill in the shape of the helmet. Start at the red line and paint in lines up to the hair.

6. Paint a black line around the red shape. Add a black line for a chinstrap, under the chin.

9

Around your eyes

It's very tickly being face painted. Try to get your model to sit as still as he can, especially when you are painting around his eyes. Always tell your model to close his eyes whenever you paint near them.

Superhero

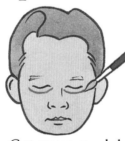

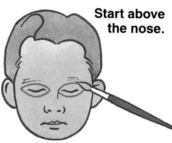

Start above the nose.

1. Get your model to close his eyes. Paint a curved line carefully under each eye, like this.

2. Paint another line over each eye just under the eyebrow. Make the lines meet at the ends.

3. Starting above the nose, paint a pointy line over the left eyebrow. Repeat it over the right eye.

When the paint is dry, squeeze a little glitter paint onto your hand. Paint it onto the pointy shapes.

Add some glitter paint on the nose too.

4. Starting on the nose, paint a pointy line across each cheek. Join the ends to the line over the eyes.

5. Use a thicker brush to fill inside your outline with neat, even brush strokes.

Carnival mask

Use a clean brush for glitter paint.

1. With red paint on a thin brush, paint a curved line above and below one of your model's eyes.

2. Starting near the top of the nose, paint a line onto the cheek, then up to the side of the face.

3. Add two lines over the eye to complete a diamond. Fill it in. Do the same in black around the other eye.

4. With gold glitter, paint an upside-down triangle on the forehead between the diamonds.

Leave a gap between the shapes.

5. Add a red, gold, black and white curved shape at each corner of the diamonds, like this.

6. Paint a white outline from the tip of the nose around the face and across the forehead.

Use a fine brush to add thin curly ribbons at each side of the mask.

7. Fill in between all the shapes with white paint. Add little black dots around the outside.

Shading and stipple

As well as using a brush, you can also use a sponge to put on face paint.

Different types of sponges, such as a stipple sponge, give you different effects. You can buy one from most costume shops or theatrical suppliers.

A stipple sponge makes speckles.

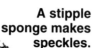

Shading with a sponge

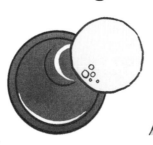

If you get streaks, your sponge is too wet.

1. Wet a make-up sponge, then squeeze it as hard as you can. Rub it in circles in your face paint.

2. Dab the sponge on the skin. Twist it a little as you do it. Don't try to smear the paint on.

3. To get a shaded look, dab lightly around the edges, with very little paint on your sponge.

Using a stipple sponge

1. Wet the sponge, then squeeze out as much water as you can. Rub it around in your face paint.

2. Dab the sponge on the back of your hand to test the paint. Do it lightly to get tiny speckles.

If you get blobs, the sponge is too wet. Squeeze it in a paper towel and rub it in the paint again.

Jolly pirate

Start in the middle each time.

1. Rub a make-up sponge in red. Dab it lightly down each cheek to make a big, bright patch.

2. Paint an arch over each eyebrow. Add more feathery lines below, as far down as the eyebrow.

3. Dip a stipple sponge in black. Dab it from each ear to the chin and across the top lip.

Make-up sponges make a smooth pattern.

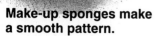

Wicked pirate

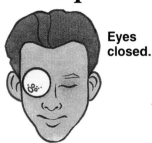

Eyes closed.

Use a thick brush.

1. Rub a make-up sponge in black. Dab it very lightly on the eyebrows and under the eyes.

2. Starting above the nose, paint a thick line down to the end of the eyebrow, then up over it.

3. With a thin brush, paint feathery lines along the top and bottom of each of the thick lines.

4. Paint a line from the top lip up to the side of the nose. Then curl it out across the cheek.

5. Paint a line along the top of the lip and out to the side. Fill in the shape and add a thin, curly end.

Sponging all over

Many faces have a layer of paint covering the whole face. This is called a base. You can brush a different shade of face paint on top of a base, once it is dry. If some paint gets on your model's hair, don't worry. Face paint washes out easily.

Putting on a base

Rub more paint on your sponge from time to time.

1. Rub a damp make-up sponge in face paint. Rub it lightly around and around in the paint.

2. Press the sponge on one cheek and twist your hand a little. Lift the sponge and dab it on again.

3. Sponge the paint across the face before it has time to dry. This gives a smooth look.

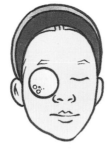

Night sky

4. To sponge under the eyes, get your model to look up. Dab very gently and carefully.

5. You need to sponge the eyelids as well. Get your model to close her eyes as you do this.

1. Press lots of self-adhesive stars onto your model's cheeks and forehead. Put one on the nose.

2. Rub a sponge around in blue. Dab it all over to make a base. Dab over the top of all the stars.

Take the paint right up to the hairline and out to the sides of the face.

3. Put some gold paint onto a brush and paint around the lips. Fill the lips in with the paint.

4. When the blue base is dry, slip a fingernail under a point on each star and pull it off.

For a link to a website where you can find pictures of flags of the world that you can copy to paint your face, go to **www.usborne-quicklinks.com**

Moon face

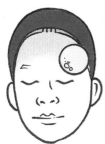 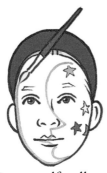 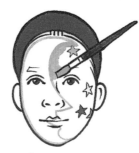 

1. Rub a sponge around in white. Dab it all over to make a base. Allow the base to dry.

2. Press self-adhesive stars down one side of the face. Paint a blue outline of a half moon, as above.

3. Brush paint out from the blue line onto the starry side. Then, fill the rest in with a sponge.

4. Paint a curved eyebrow. Add a line from the nose to the lip. Pull off the stars when the base is dry.

Add a little gold glitter spray. Get your model to close her eyes when you use it.

Cover your hair with blue spray. Cover your face as you spray.

Mix the blue as light or as dark as you like.

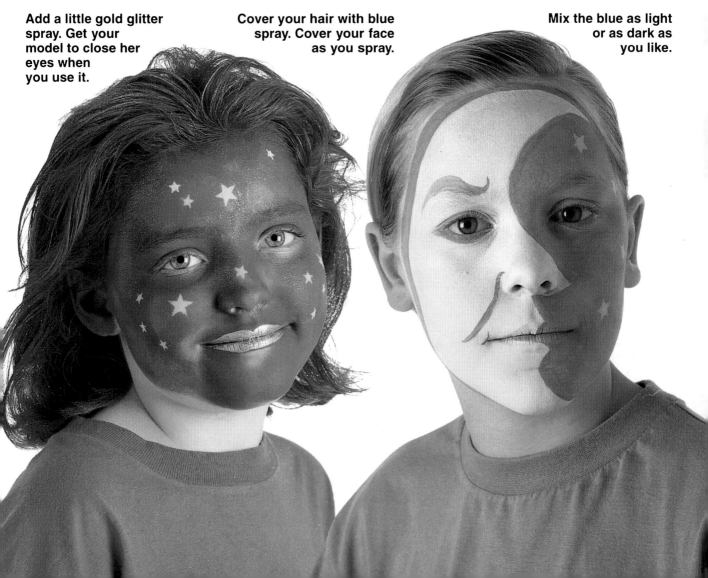

Brush marks

For a link to a website where you can find some exciting ideas for painting your face like a Native American from the 19th century, go to **www.usborne-quicklinks.com**

When the base on your model's face has dried, you can sponge or brush more paint on top. You can do lines, spots or dots, or you can use the side of your brush to make shapes. These can be turned into all kinds of things, such as flowers or fish.

Dip your brush in water, then roll it around in paint so that the bristles are completely covered.

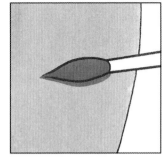

Instead of painting with the tip of the brush, gently lay the bristles flat on the skin, then lift it off.

A thin, pointed brush

A fat, flat-ended brush

A fat, pointed brush

The shape you make with the paint depends on the shape of the brush you are using.

Flowers

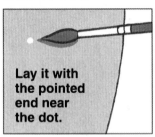

Lay it with the pointed end near the dot.

Paint a dot. To make a petal, put paint onto a thin, pointed brush and lay it flat on the face.

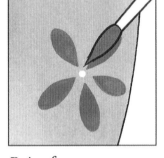

Paint four more petals around the dot in the same way. Space them as evenly as you can.

For a two-tone petal, dip your brush in one shade of paint, then dip just the tip in a different one.

To make the petals of a flower look the same, do them all without adding more paint to your brush.

Leaves

Put green on your brush. To make a leaf, put your brush on the face with its tip at the bottom.

Lift your brush and paint another leaf beside the first one. Add one more below them.

Fish

Add an eye when the paint is dry.

Lay the bristles of a pointed brush flat on the face. Use the tip of it to add two marks for the tail.

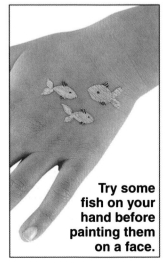

Try some fish on your hand before painting them on a face.

Flower face

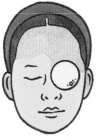

1. Sponge a bright yellow base all over your model's face (see page 14). Stop just before the hair.

Space out the spots.

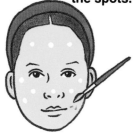

2. Paint three white spots across the forehead and on each cheek. Paint one on the nose too.

Brush orange face paint onto your lips.

3. Dip a clean brush into orange and roll it around, then dip just the tip into white paint.

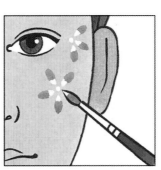

4. Paint five petals around each white spot by laying the bristles flat on the face (see left).

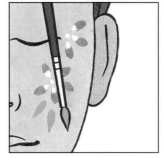

5. Clean your brush and dip it in green. Add leaves between the petals by laying your brush flat.

Start in the middle.

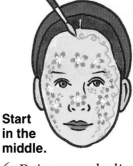

6. Paint a curly line around the face. Do one side, then do the other. The sides don't need to match.

Moving pictures

By opening and closing your mouth, you can make this shark's jaws bite.

You may not have all the paints that you need for this face, but don't worry. You can mix face paints together in the same way as you mix ordinary paint.

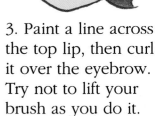

1. Sponge a pale blue base all over the face. Make a smooth edge under the chin.

2. While the base is drying, mix a little white and black paint to make grey (see right).

3. Paint a line across the top lip, then curl it over the eyebrow. Try not to lift your brush as you do it.

Use a thin brush.

4. To make the shark's tail, paint a line around the eye and back to the first line you painted.

5. For the head, do a line out from the mouth. Take it round under the nose and up to meet the tail.

6. Fill in the shape you have made. Paint a curved fin by the side of the nose and fill it in too.

7. Take a line under the bottom lip, up to join the tail. Fill in the shape you've made with white.

8. When the lips are dry, use grey on a thin brush to paint zigzag lines for sharp teeth.

9. Clean the brush, then paint red along the inside of the teeth, on both lips. Add a white eye.

10. Paint grey curved lines on the body for gills. Add some dots on the shark's side.

11. Add some fish by laying a brush flat (see page 24). Add thin green lines for seaweed.

18

Mixing paint

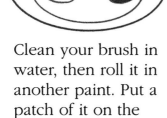

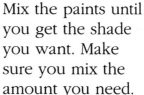

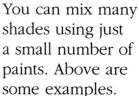

To make a different shade, dip your brush in one paint, then brush it on an old saucer or plate.

This is the effect that you get as you open your mouth.

Clean your brush in water, then roll it in another paint. Put a patch of it on the saucer too.

Use a straw to add bubbles (see page 9).

Mix the paints until you get the shade you want. Make sure you mix the amount you need.

You can mix many shades using just a small number of paints. Above are some examples.

Animal faces

When you're painting details on a face, it's a good idea to start at the top and work down. So, start with the eyebrows and do the mouth last.

If you don't have the shade of paint you need for the base, you can mix it with a sponge (see below).

Bear

Mix the paint on your hand if you need to.

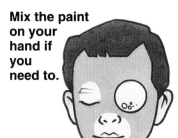

1. Sponge a base over the face. Leave bare patches around the mouth and nose, and over the eyes.

2. Get your model to close his eyes and mouth, then sponge the bare patches with a paler shade.

3. Brush a dark brown arch shape over each eyebrow. Add a smaller arch above them.

Add black dots and whiskers.

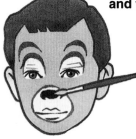

4. Paint a brown line around the nose and mouth. Paint the end of the nose and nostrils with black.

5. Paint an upside-down 'V' from the nose to the top lip. Fill in the bottom lip and add 'smile' lines.

Paint a thin white line along each whisker to make it stand out.

Mixing paint with a sponge

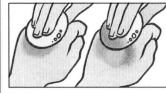

Add yellow and white for the eyes and muzzle.

Rub your sponge in orange paint, then rub it onto the back of your hand.

Dab the other side of the sponge in brown paint, then mix it on your hand.

For a link to a website where you can find simple outlines of
animal faces to copy, go to **www.usborne-quicklinks.com**

Mouse

1. Sponge a lilac base over the face. Leave bare patches over the eyes and around the mouth.

2. Sponge the bare patches with white. Go over the edge of each patch so that you get a soft effect.

3. Sponge a darker lilac on the cheeks and forehead. Paint pink eyebrows (see step 3 of the bear).

4. Paint the tip of the nose pink.

Add the teeth when the pink on the bottom lip is dry.

5. Paint a line from the nose to the top lip. Fill in the bottom lip. Add dots, white whiskers and teeth.

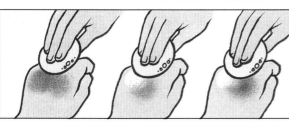

For lilac, use purple or a mixture of red and blue. Add white to make it lilac.

If you don't have pink face paint, you can mix red and white.

21

Shiny face paints

You can buy different kinds of shiny face paints. Mix them with water in the same way as ordinary face paint (see page 4). You can also get shiny powder, called irridescent powder. Use this on a dry brush.

Use glitter paint to add some sparkly lines (see page 6).

Use hair gel and glitter paint in your hair too.

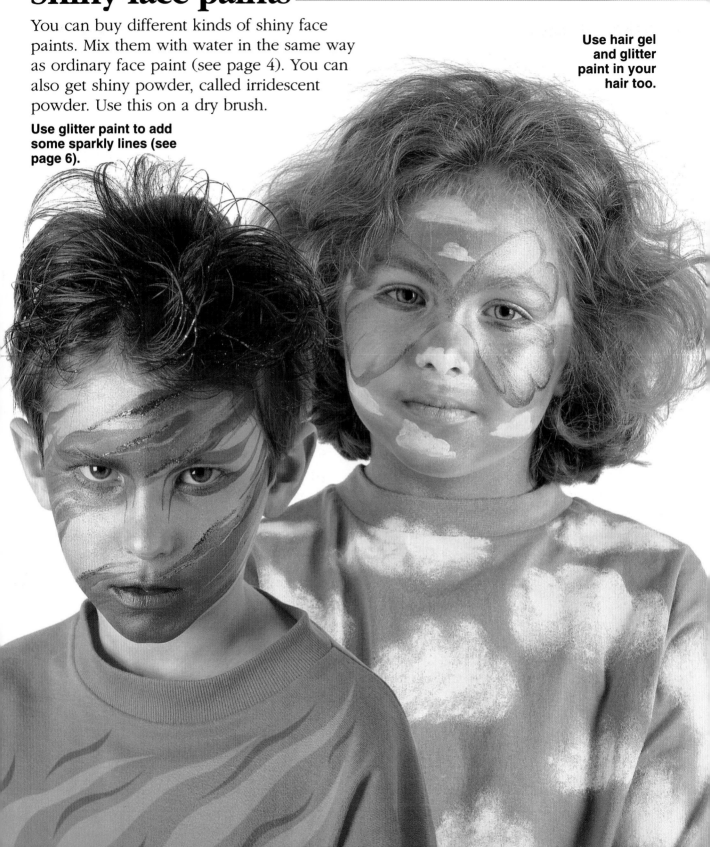

Golden wings

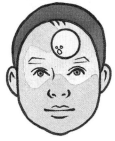 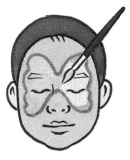 

1. Sponge blue paint over the face, but leave a bare patch around the eyes, for the wings.

2. Starting above the nose, paint a bronze wing shape around the bare patch. Fill it with gold.

3. Paint white cloud shapes on the forehead, nose and chin. Do some on the cheeks too.

Fire face

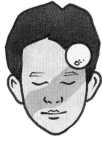 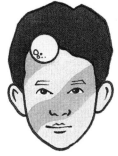 

1. Rub your sponge in gold and dab a wide stripe from the jaw across the face, to above the ear.

2. Add another stripe of gold across the forehead. Start by the ear and sponge right up to the hair.

3. Sponge a bronze stripe between the gold ones. Do another stripe across the chin to the ear.

4. With red or gold on your brush, paint some flame shapes. Follow the angle of the stripes.

5. Paint a dark brown line along each eyebrow. Add a curved line along the bottom eyelids.

6. Use a thin brush to continue the lines down the side of the nose. Make the other ends curve up.

Shiny paints

Bronze paint

Gold paint

Brush irridescent powder over the top of a painted area to make it shiny.

Add glitter paint too (see page 6).

Mix pearly paints with water. Brush or sponge them on.

23

Blending paints

When you sponge one paint over another, you mix the paints and get a new shade. This is called blending. Not all shades of paint blend well together. Blue and orange, for instance, make muddy brown. Try to use shades that are similar.

Squeeze out as much water from your sponge as you can before you rub it in the face paint.

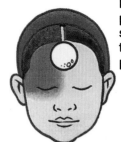

Dab on a patch of paint. Make it less dense around the edges where you're going to blend.

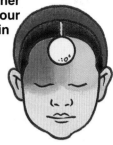

Dip another part of your sponge in the next paint.

Dab on another patch. Press lightly were the paints overlap so that they blend together.

You could paint a gold sun on the forehead.

Rainbow face

1. Beginning with pink paint, then turquoise, blend patches around the face, like this.

2. With blue, paint a line along each eyebrow. Use a thin brush to make a curly end.

Look up.

3. Paint a line under each eye. Add three wiggly lines from the line down each cheek.

Paint the lips too.

4. Add raindrops on the cheeks. To make the drops look shiny, leave a part of each one unpainted.

Fish face

Eyes closed.

1. With yellow on your sponge, dab a circular patch like this. Let it fade around the edge.

2. Dab blue around the face. It will go green where it blends with the yellow.

3. Paint a thin blue line down the forehead. Add thick lines from it. Join them with thin lines.

4. Paint a line along the bottom of each eye. Take the line around the eye to make a big circle.

To make the blue lines show up, paint inside each one with gold.

Paint the lips too.

Notice how the the blue and the yellow paint blend evenly together to make green.

5. Paint four lines on each cheek. Join the ends to make a fin shape. Add curved scale shapes all over.

Changing the shape of your face

You can change the shape of your face by painting lines and sponging light and dark patches with your face paints. Follow these instructions to paint either an ice queen or king. For a king, add a beard, like the one in the photograph.

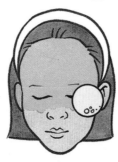

1. Rub a damp sponge in blue paint and sponge a base over your model's face, up to the hair.

2. Rub your sponge in white and press it lightly across the forehead and along the cheekbones.

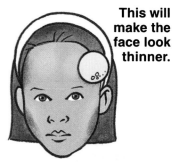

This will make the face look thinner.

3. Sponge dark blue from the jaw, down the side of the face. Add some at the side of the forehead.

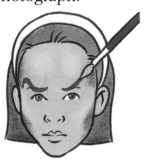

4. Starting above the nose, paint a line over each eyebrow. Curve it up, then down and up a little.

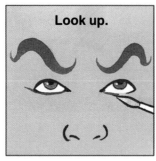

Look up.

5. With a thin brush, starting at the nose paint a line under each eye. Curve up the end of the line.

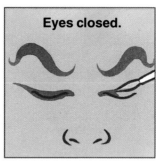

Eyes closed.

6. Paint a thick line across each eyelid. Join the ends of the line to the one below the eye.

7. Starting on the line under the eye, paint a thin line down each side of the nose.

8. Paint thin lines from the eyebrows up onto the forehead, and down the side of the nose.

Paint the lips blue.

9. Add a line from the top of the jaw, around the bottom of the cheekbone, and down the face.

10. Get your model to wrinkle her nose. Paint a line down the two deep creases beside the mouth.

11. To make your nose more pointed, paint a line from the bottom of the nose, around each nostril.

Paint the ice king's beard with small downward brushstrokes.

Only the bottom lip on the ice king is painted dark blue. This makes the top lip look longer.

If you have shiny face paint or powder (see page 25), dab some under the eyebrows.

Fur effect

You can paint fur-like patterns on an animal face by using the side of your brush (see page 16) and overlapping your brushstrokes. This face looks complicated as it has so many steps, but it's not too difficult. You don't need to get the patterns on both sides of the face to match exactly.

All the fur markings on this face were painted with the side of a thin brush.

Wild cat

1. Sponge on a light brown base. Leave bare patches around the eyes, mouth and chin, like this.

2. Sponge reddish brown across the forehead and down the nose. Add a little on the cheeks too.

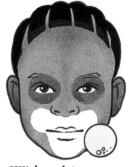

3. With white, sponge the bare patch around the mouth and onto the cheeks and chin.

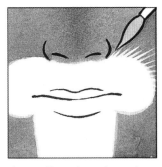

4. Roll a thin brush in white and paint feathery lines out from white patches on the cheeks.

Get your model to look up.

5. Paint a thick white line under each eye. Add a line from the corner of the eye, up over each eyebrow.

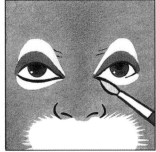

6. With black on a thin brush, very carefully paint a line along the bottom lid of each eye.

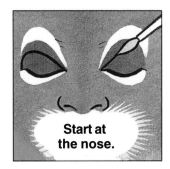

Start at the nose.

7. Add a line on the top lid by going up to the eyebrow and then around to the corner of the eye.

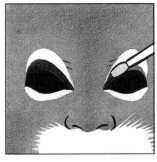

8. Fill in the top lid with black. Paint a dark brown line between the lid and the top white line.

Use a thin brush.

9. At the end of the brown line, use the side of your brush to make long marks. Overlap them a little.

10. Use the side of your brush to make brown fur patterns down the forehead and onto the nose.

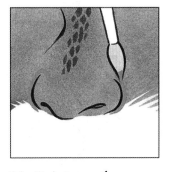

11. Paint up the crease on each side of the nose to meet on top. Fill in the tip of the nose with pink.

12. Use the side of your brush again to add black fur marks over each eyebrow and on the forehead.

13. Paint black lines from the eyes around the nose. Add a line on the top lip and fill the lips in too.

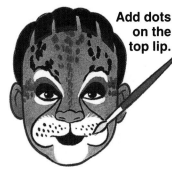

Add dots on the top lip.

14. Paint a black line from the corner of each eye around the white patches on the cheeks.

15. Add more fur marks below the eyes, across the cheeks and around the mouth and chin.

29

More ideas

Clown

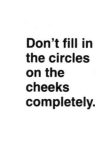

Don't fill in the circles on the cheeks completely.

1. Sponge on a white base. When it is dry, paint black triangles below the eyes. Add pointed eyebrows.

2. Paint a circle on each cheek. Join them to the lips. Paint the lips, taking the bottom one onto the chin.

Robot

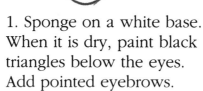

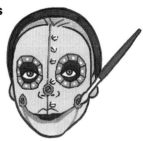

Add screws with a big straw (see page 9).

1. Sponge on a gold base. Outline the eyes with black. Paint another line around them. Fill in with bronze.

2. Paint a line down the face and top lip. Add a bolt on the nose and cheeks. Paint in a large mouth.

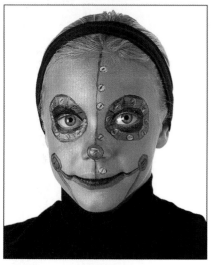

Dalmation

Decorate the face with whiskers and spots.

1. Sponge a white base. Paint a thin line under each eye. Add a patch and an eyebrow over the eyes.

2. Add red tongue. Paint the nose black. Take a line onto the top lip and fill it in. Outline the tongue.

Hatching duck

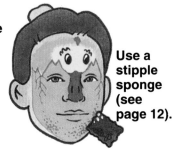

Sponge pink on the forehead.

Use a stipple sponge (see page 12).

1. For the eggshell, paint a zigzag across the forehead and around the nose. Sponge blue below the line.

2. For a beak, paint the nose orange. Paint a yellow head and big eyes. Add cracks and stipple on the shell.

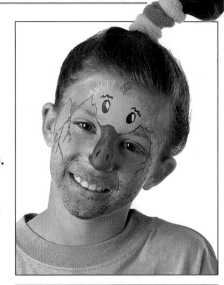

Lion

Add orange whiskers and a red bottom lip.

1. Sponge on a pale orange base, leaving a bare patch on the cheeks and chin. Fill the patch in with white.

2. Sponge white over each eye and outline it with black. Paint black on the eyes, nose and top lip.

Snake

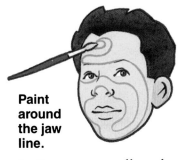

Paint around the jaw line.

Paint the lips red.

1. Sponge a yellow base. With green on a thin brush, paint an outline which curls around the face, like this.

2. For eyes, paint red, then white, around the nostrils. Fill in the snake with gold, green and black patterns.

Index

Suppliers and information

To find face paint suppliers, look at 'Costume shops' or 'Theatrical suppliers' in your yellow pages telephone directory. Call them and ask if they sell water-based face paints. Some toy stores also sell them. For further information about face painting, contact this international organization:-

FACE,
The Face Painting Assocation,
Rookery Barn, Sandpit Lane,
Bledlow, Princes Risborough,
Buckinghamshire
HP27 9QQ
United Kingdom

With thanks to: Katie Aggett, Asher Edge Blake, Nicole Cason-Marcus, Thomas and David Edwards, Justine and Gabrielle Fisher, Tashi and Lucas Giffard Petter, Chloe and Lucy Goldsmith, Emily-Rose and Edward Goldsmith, Patrick Harding, Christine Johnson, Tatsuya and Shunya Kurokawa, Kattja Madrell, Taniya Noble, Xan-Carlos and Rui-Blas Perez-Lopez, Lorraine and Richard Reeves, Jessica Roberts, Katelyn Stanwick, Francesca and Peter Wormald.

Additional Research by Liz Dalby and Rachel Firth.